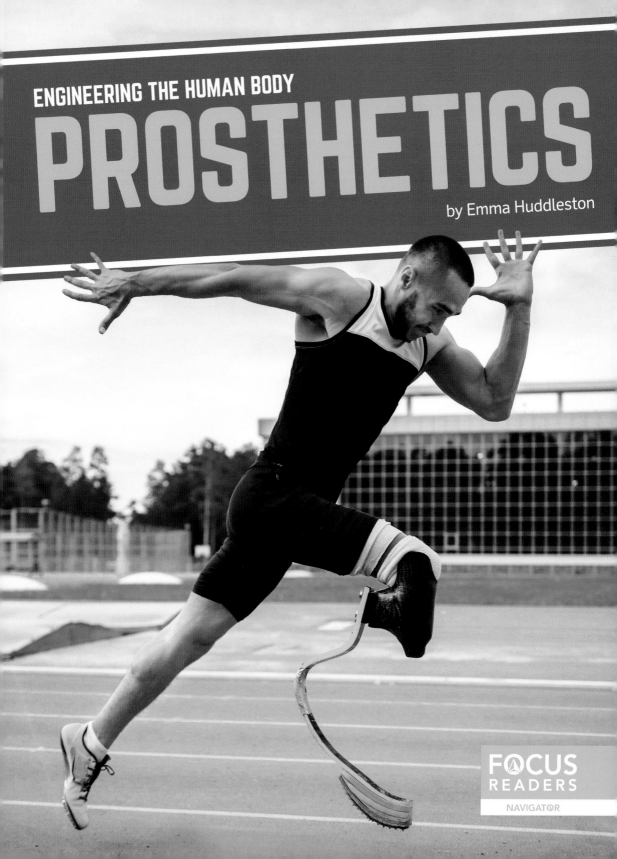

ENGINEERING THE HUMAN BODY

PROSTHETICS

by Emma Huddleston

FOCUS
READERS

NAVIGATOR

WWW.FOCUSREADERS.COM

Focus Readers is distributed by North Star Editions:
sales@northstareditions.com | 888-417-0195

Produced for Focus Readers by Red Line Editorial.

Content Consultant: Richard Weir, Research Associate Professor of Bioengineering, University of Colorado, Denver

Photographs ©: sportpoint/Shutterstock Images, cover, 1; Stephanie Yao Long/The Oregonian/AP Images, 4–5; Sharomka/Shutterstock Images, 7; Dean Drobot/Shutterstock Images, 9; Life Magazine/AP Images, 10–11; JohnnyGreig/iStockphoto, 13; Red Line Editorial, 15; Medicimage/UIG Universal Images Group/Newscom, 17; Czgur/iStockphoto, 18–19; CP DC Press/Shutterstock Images, 21; Shizuo Kambayashi/AP Images, 23; SeventyFour/Shutterstock Images, 24–25; Dima Gavrysh/AP Images, 27; Kyodo/AP Images, 28

Library of Congress Cataloging-in-Publication Data
Names: Huddleston, Emma, author.
Title: Prosthetics / by Emma Huddleston.
Description: Lake Elmo, MN : Focus Readers, [2020] | Series:
  Engineering the human body | Audience: Grades 4 to 6. | Includes
  bibliographical references and index.
Identifiers: LCCN 2018054458 (print) | LCCN 2018058970 (ebook) | ISBN
  9781641859745 (pdf) | ISBN 9781641859059 (e-book) | ISBN 9781641857673
  (hardcover) | ISBN 9781641858366 (pbk.)
Subjects: LCSH: Prosthesis--Juvenile literature. | Prosthesis--Technological
  innovations--Juvenile literature.
Classification: LCC RD130 (ebook) | LCC RD130 .H83 2020 (print) | DDC
  617.9/56--dc23
LC record available at https://lccn.loc.gov/2018054458

Printed in the United States of America
Mankato, MN
May, 2019

ABOUT THE AUTHOR

Emma Huddleston lives in Minnesota's Twin Cities with her husband. She enjoys writing children's books, but she likes reading novels even more. When she is not writing or reading, she stays active by running and swing dancing.

TABLE OF CONTENTS

CHAPTER 1

MOVING IN NEW WAYS

Angel Giuffria was born without a left hand. Her arm ends just below the left elbow. She received her first **prosthesis** when she was six weeks old. From then on, she wore a prosthetic hand every day.

Her old prosthesis had limited abilities. The thumb and the fingers could press together. But that was it.

A boy practices picking up a water bottle using his new prosthetic arm.

In 2014, Giuffria received a new prosthetic hand. It lets her grasp things in a new way. A socket fits over her left elbow. A hand made of metal, rubber, and plastic fits into the socket. The socket senses the movements of her arm muscles. It responds by sending instructions to five motors in the palm of the hand. The fingers of the hand curl.

Over time, Giuffria learned how to use her new hand. She can curl one finger at a time. She can cook, lift weights, and tie her shoelaces. She can pursue her interest in acting and modeling.

People look at her artificial hand. But Giuffria has never felt ashamed about it.

Many people who have been injured during military service use prostheses.

She likes talking to people about what her hand can do.

Prostheses replace missing body parts. Most people think of artificial limbs when they think of prostheses. But even false teeth and artificial eyes are prostheses.

There are two main types of artificial limbs. They are upper limb and lower limb. Upper-limb prostheses can be above the elbow or below the elbow. Lower-limb prostheses can be above the knee or below the knee. Each type has challenges.

One challenge with prosthetic arms is creating an alternative for the hand. Hands have many tiny muscles and can perform detailed tasks. It is difficult to use an artificial limb in the same way.

Balance and strength are challenges for prosthetic legs. Even standing can be hard. Above-knee prostheses are especially tricky. The knee joint has a key role in walking. But it is hard to copy.

Prostheses allow people who have lost lower limbs to stay active.

People can be missing a limb for many reasons. Some people are born without one. Others have a limb removed due to sickness or injury. It is not easy to live with a missing limb. Prostheses can help make it easier.

CHAPTER 2

IMPROVING PROSTHESES

People have been using prostheses for thousands of years. Wooden legs are some of the oldest examples. These legs were uncomfortable and heavy. Prosthetic technology improved greatly in the 1900s. New prostheses were made with lighter materials, such as plastic. They were more comfortable to wear.

After World War II (1939–1945), many wounded soldiers needed prostheses.

New prostheses had several connected pieces. These pieces allowed the limbs to bend. Prostheses improved in appearance as well. Some looked like real body parts. They matched people's skin color. They could even have freckles.

Today, prostheses can be made with carbon fiber. This material is as strong

GETTING USED TO IT

People have to **adjust** to life with a prosthesis. Many people who use prostheses go to physical therapy. They learn to move their muscles in new ways. They practice wearing and using their new prostheses. Prostheses are an amazing technology. But they are not the same as natural body parts. Adjusting to them takes time.

Physical therapists teach people how to use their prostheses.

as metal and as light as plastic. It makes prostheses easier to use.

People who make prostheses must take careful measurements. All bodies are different. The size of limbs varies. Prostheses work best when they fit well.

Most prostheses have several parts. These parts are usually made of different materials. The most common materials are plastic, metal, rubber, foam, and carbon fiber.

One important part of a prosthesis is the socket. It is the part that meets the person's body. The socket is usually made of plastic. The plastic socket can take any shape. Doctors bend and mold the plastic to fit the patient. Another important part is the pylon. This part replaces the person's bone. It is usually made of metal or carbon fiber.

An outside cover makes a prosthesis look like a real body part. It can be made from foam or rubber. Some people choose not to have a cover. Prostheses can be many shapes and sizes. Each one is unique.

PARTS OF A PROSTHESIS

Several parts make up a prosthetic leg. One is the optional foam cover. It is covered with artificial skin to look like a natural leg.

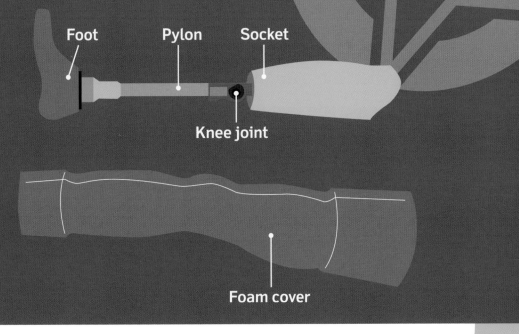

Foot   Pylon   Socket

Knee joint

Foam cover

USING PROSTHETIC DEVICES

Not all prosthetic devices work in the same way. Some prostheses are powered by the body. For instance, an upper-limb prosthesis might require a harness. A harness is a set of cables that a person wears across his or her shoulders. The cables connect to a prosthetic hand. When the person raises his or her shoulders, the cables pull upward. This movement causes the prosthetic hand to open. When the person relaxes the shoulders, the hand closes. The feeling of the cable against the shoulders tells the person if the hand is open or closed.

Lower-limb prostheses work differently. One example is an **exoskeleton**. This type of prosthesis straps onto a person's leg. It helps the

This prosthetic hand is operated using a harness placed around the opposite shoulder.

person walk. The device is partly powered by the person's muscles. But it is also partly robotic. It helps straighten the knee as the person walks.

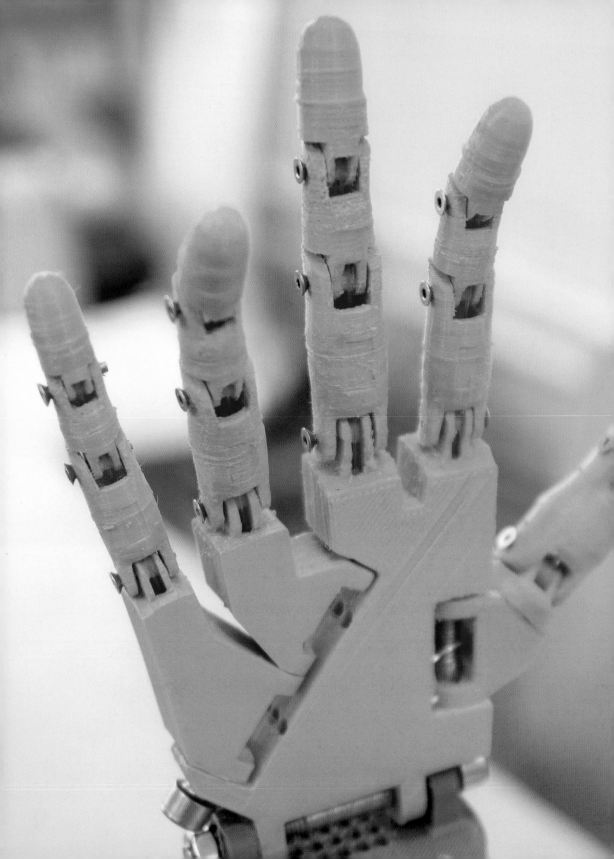

CHAPTER 3

PROSTHESES IN THE REAL WORLD

Many people use prostheses. Lusie was born with a missing limb. Her arm stops right below her elbow. She uses a plastic 3D-printed prosthesis. It is lightweight and comfortable. It has straps that go around the shoulders. Lusie controls the prosthesis with her elbow. One day, she hopes to do a cartwheel.

A hand is a complex body part to mimic because of its many muscles and abilities.

Jerome Singleton is a runner. He is a member of the US Paralympic track team. The Paralympic Games is a sports event for athletes who have disabilities. Singleton's leg was removed below the knee when he was a baby. But that did not stop him from running. He wanted to be the fastest Paralympic runner in the world.

Singleton uses a prosthetic leg made from carbon fiber. It helps him run quickly. At the 2008 Paralympic Games, Singleton won a gold medal in the sprint relay. He also won a silver medal in the 100-meter dash. In 2017, Singleton placed fourth in the 100-meter dash at

Jerome Singleton (far right) runs in the 2016 Rio Paralympic Games.

the World Championships. He ran the race in 11.08 seconds.

Cathy Hutchinson had a **stroke** when she was 43 years old. Afterward, she could not use her limbs. She needed help doing daily tasks. She could not eat or drink on her own. But in 2005, Hutchinson tried a new technology.

Doctors put a tiny device in her brain. They also put an advanced prosthesis on her arm. The two parts worked together. The device in her brain recorded her thoughts. Then it sent the information to the prosthesis. This technology is called a brain-machine **interface**. Hutchinson

BY THE NUMBERS

Many people have missing limbs. In the United States, for example, one in 190 people is missing a limb. By 2050, more than 3.6 million people in the United States might be missing a limb. A large part of the population is getting older. Many older people struggle with heart disease or diabetes. These illnesses can lead to limb loss.

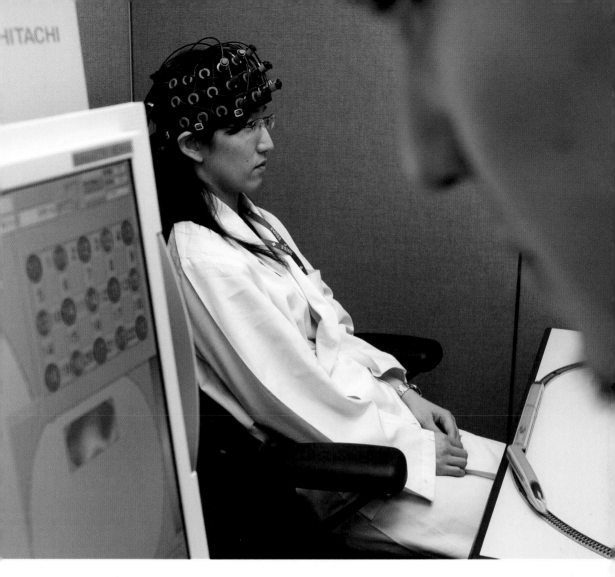

Scientists test headgear that uses a brain-machine interface.

spent years learning to use it. In 2012, she was able to drink from a cup by herself.

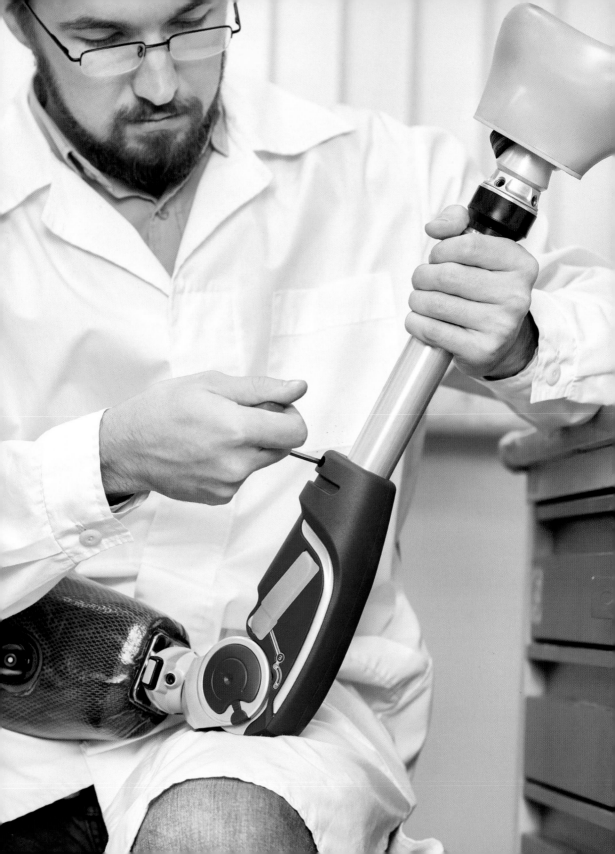

CHAPTER 4

THE FUTURE OF PROSTHETICS

Scientists are always trying to improve prostheses. They want prostheses to work like natural body parts. This means giving people more control. Many people control their prostheses using other body parts. But some people can't move their other body parts. And for some people, moving takes too much energy.

A doctor makes adjustments to a prosthetic leg.

Fortunately, there is another option for these patients. Not all prostheses are powered by the body. Some prostheses use power from **external** energy, such as batteries. That way, the person uses less energy to move the prosthesis.

One external option is a peripheral **nerve** interface. This technology allows a person's nerves to share information with a prosthesis. However, it requires surgery.

A doctor puts tiny cups on the ends of the person's nerves. These cups carry signals from the nerves to the prosthesis. The signals tell the prosthesis how to move. In this way, the prosthesis moves more naturally.

This prosthesis, called the Power Knee, moves by mimicking the motion of the person's remaining leg.

Another new technology is the myoelectric prosthesis. It has tiny **sensors** inside. The sensors receive signals from the person's muscles. When the muscles move, the sensors tell the prosthesis to move, too. The prosthesis responds to the person's body.

A girl plays a violin using a myoelectric prosthetic arm.

Every person with a missing limb has unique needs. Externally powered prostheses aren't for everyone. They can be expensive. They can also be hard to get used to. People with missing limbs must choose the prostheses that are right for them.

In the future, people will have more options than ever. However, designing prostheses takes time. New prostheses must be tested. Even then, it can take years for people to learn to use them. Thankfully, as science improves, these steps may become easier.

IN THE MAKING

One company is changing the way prostheses attach to the body. The company designed a prosthetic interface device (PID). The PID goes inside the remaining part of a person's arm or leg. It attaches to the person's bone. It also connects to the nerves. A prosthesis plugs into the PID. The PID allows the brain, body, and prosthesis to share information quickly. It may also help prevent infection.

FOCUS ON
PROSTHETICS

Write your answers on a separate piece of paper.

1. Write a paragraph summarizing the main ideas in Chapter 2.

2. Which type of prosthesis do you think would be the hardest to make? Why?

3. Which material was first used to make prostheses?

   A. plastic

   B. wood

   C. carbon fiber

4. Which prosthetic device would be best for someone without the use of his or her legs?

   A. a 3D-printed prosthesis

   B. an exoskeleton

   C. a prosthesis and harness

Answer key on page 32.

GLOSSARY

adjust
To get used to.

exoskeleton
A device strapped to and worn on the outside of the body.

external
Happening outside the body.

interface
A point at which two things meet and interact.

nerve
A long, thin fiber that carries information between the brain and other parts of the body.

prosthesis
An artificial body part.

sensors
Devices that collect and report information.

stroke
A disease that occurs when blood flow to an area of the brain is blocked.

TO LEARN MORE

BOOKS

Bethea, Nikole Brooks. *Discover Bionics*. Minneapolis: Lerner Publications, 2017.

Furstinger, Nancy. *Unstoppable: True Stories of Amazing Bionic Animals.* Boston: Houghton Mifflin Harcourt, 2017.

Kenney, Karen Latchana. *Cutting-Edge 3D Printing*. Minneapolis: Lerner Publications, 2019.

NOTE TO EDUCATORS

Visit **www.focusreaders.com** to find lesson plans, activities, links, and other resources related to this title.

WITHDRAWN

INDEX

Answer Key: 1. Answers will vary; **2.** Answers will vary; **3.** B; **4.** B